Flash & Art Stencils

2021 Big Book of Plants

JAMIE METZGER

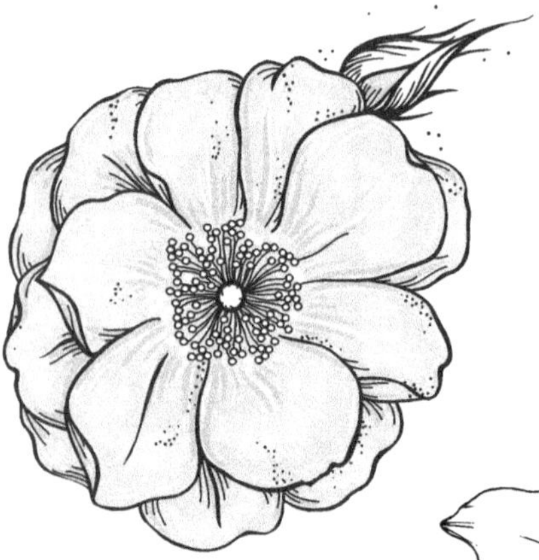
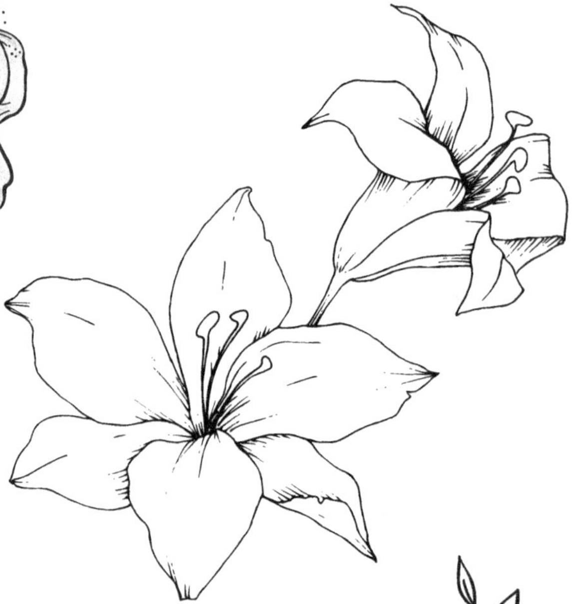
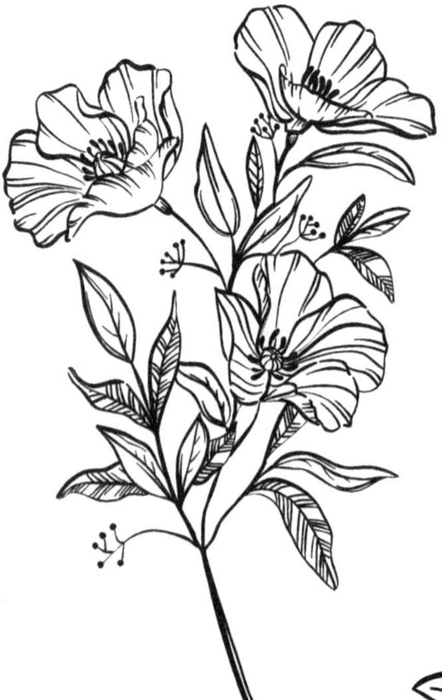
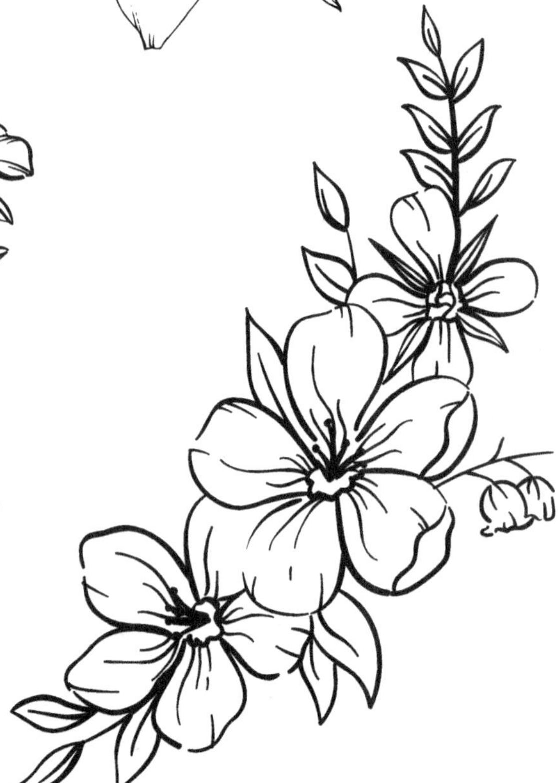

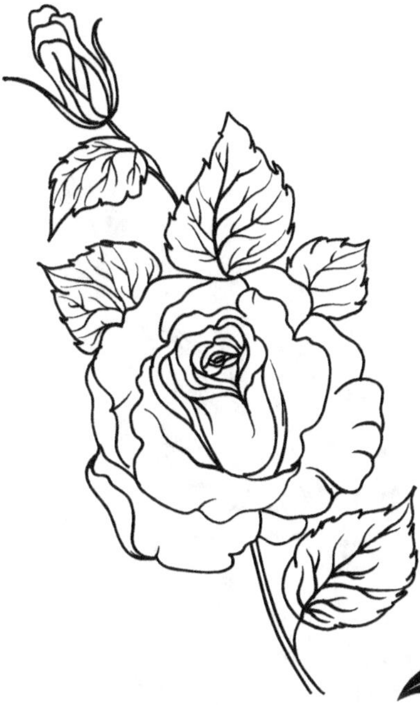

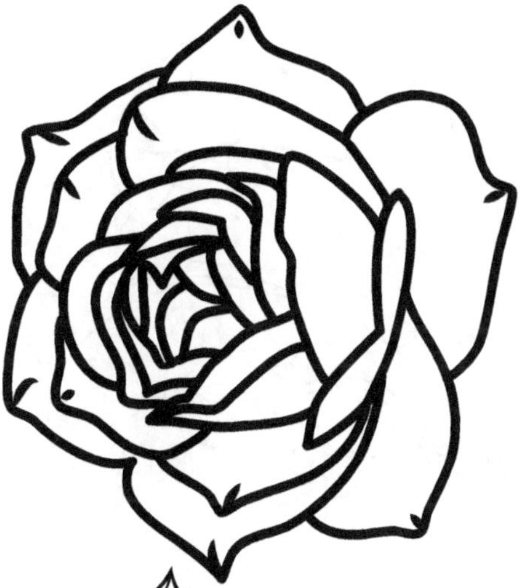

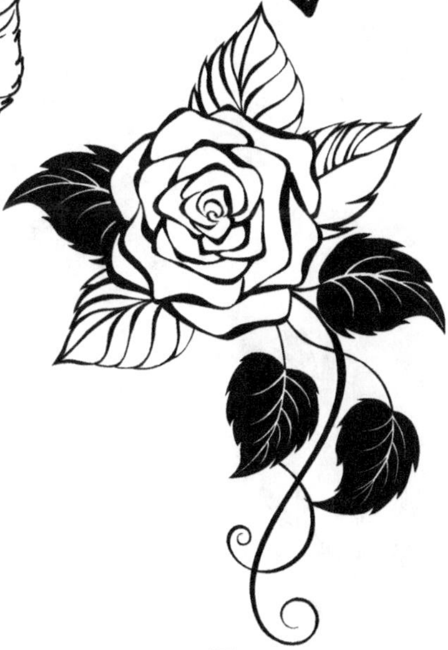

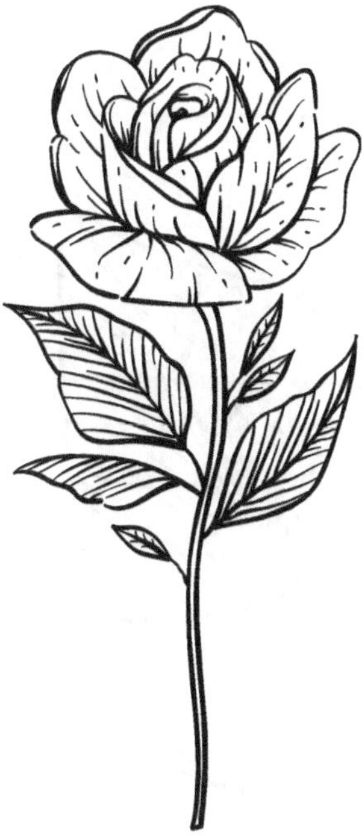

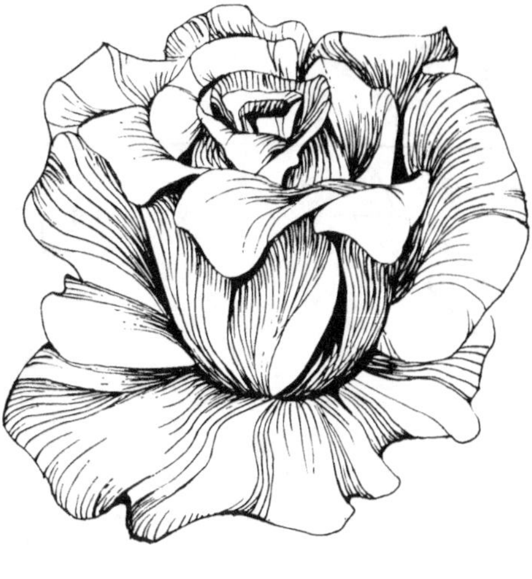

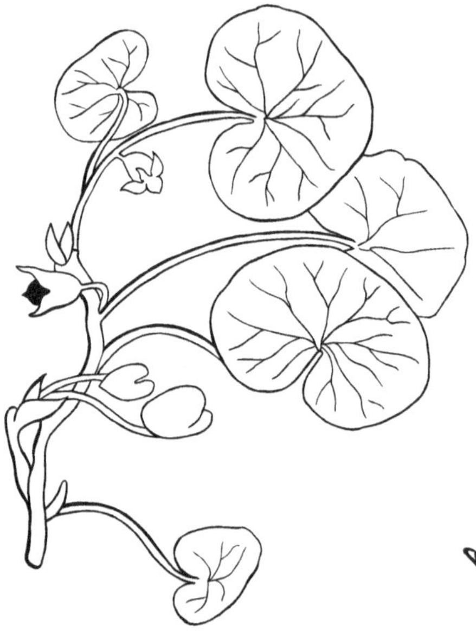

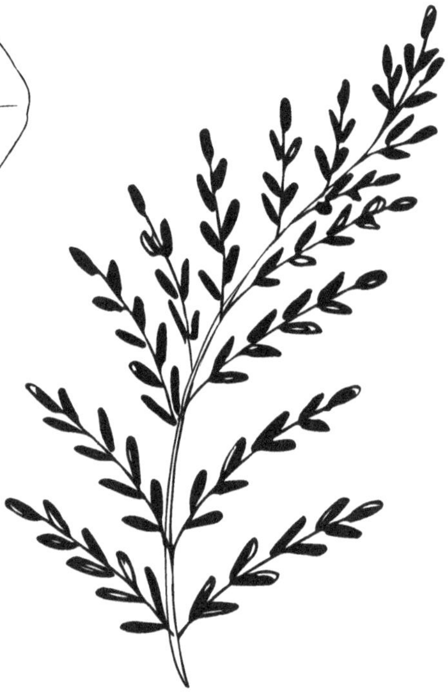

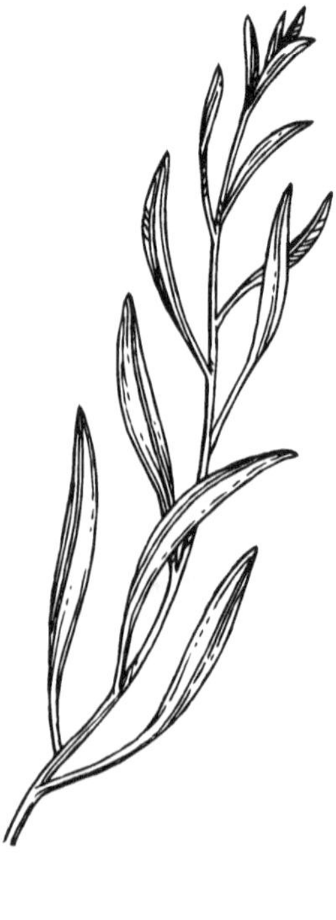

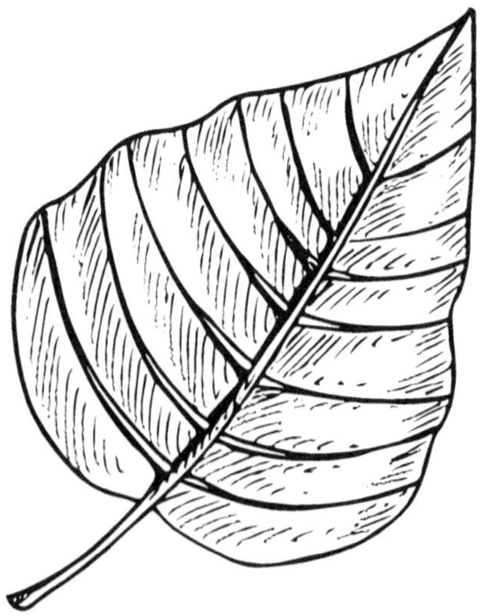

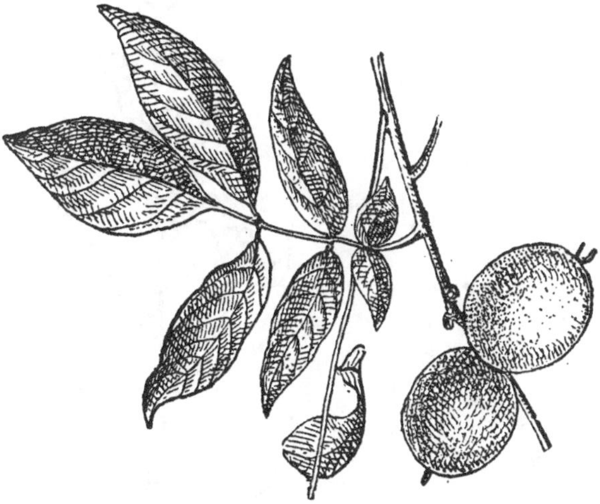

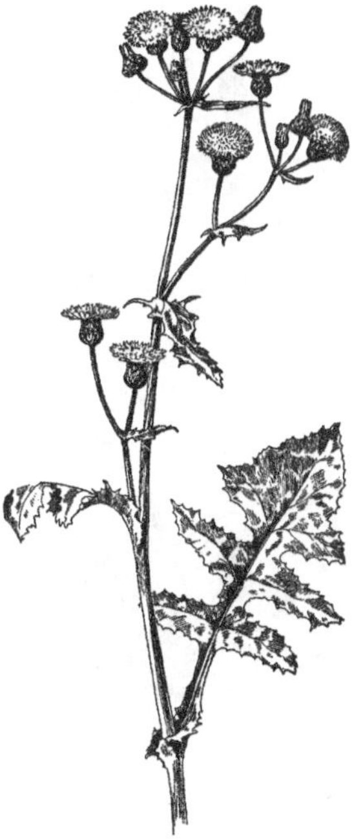

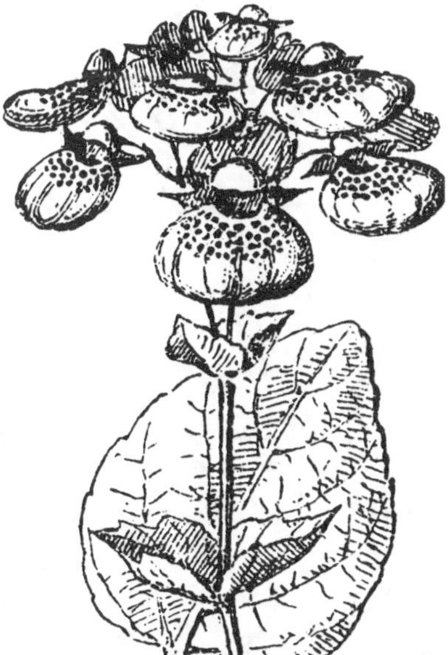

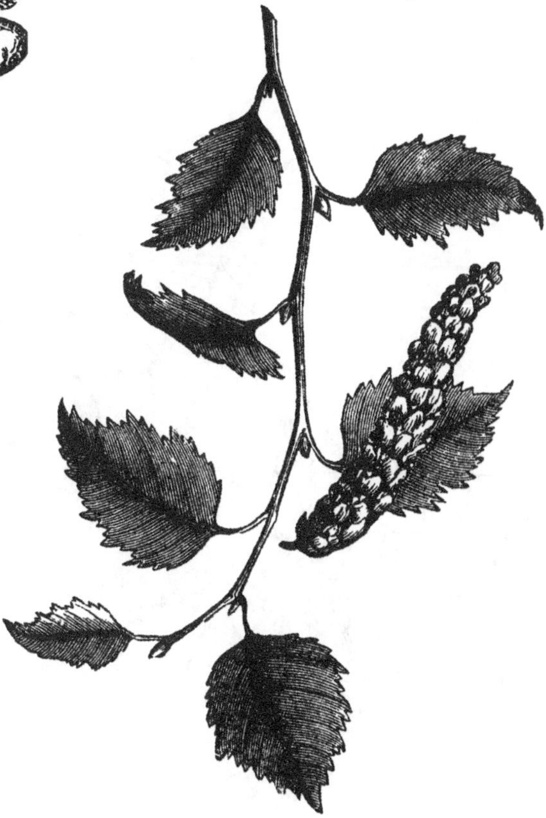

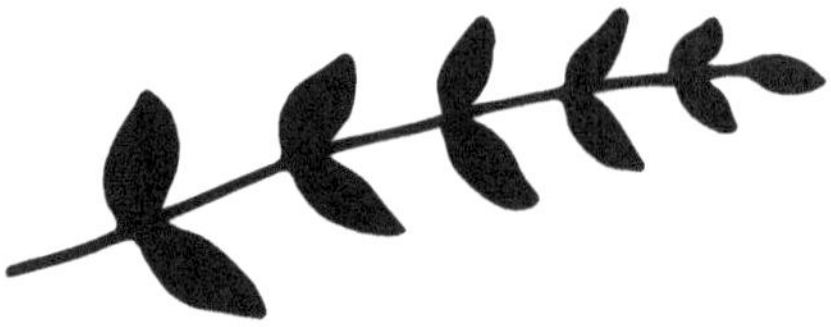
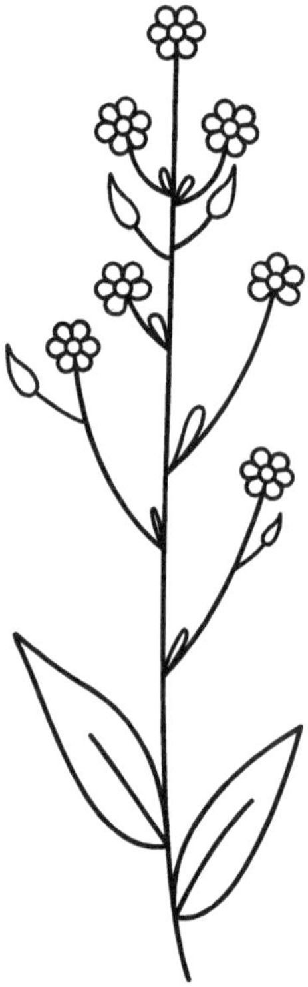
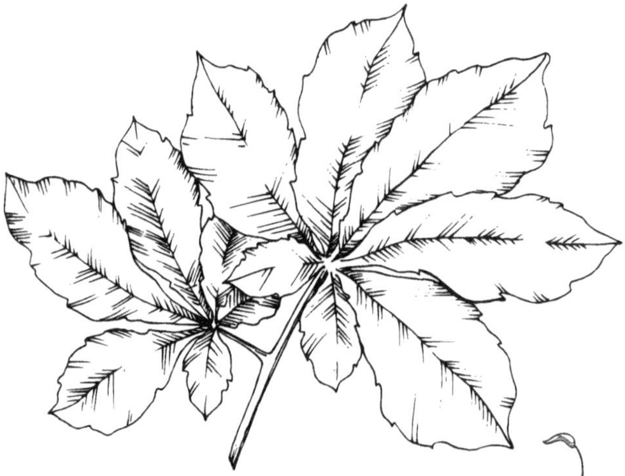
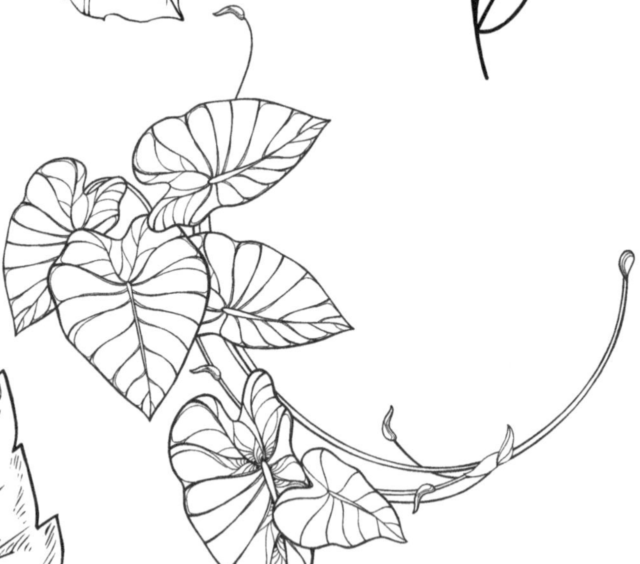
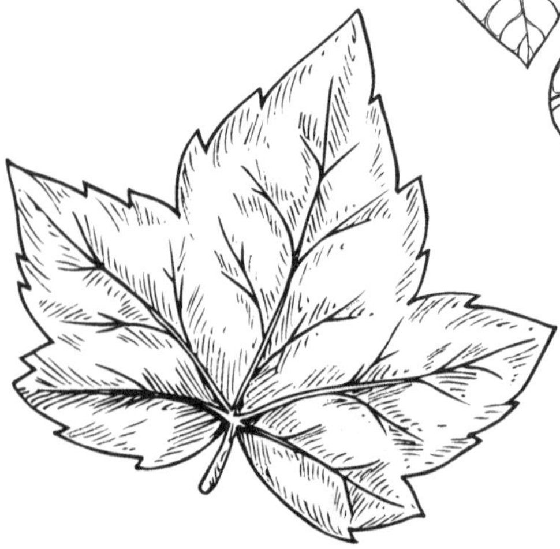

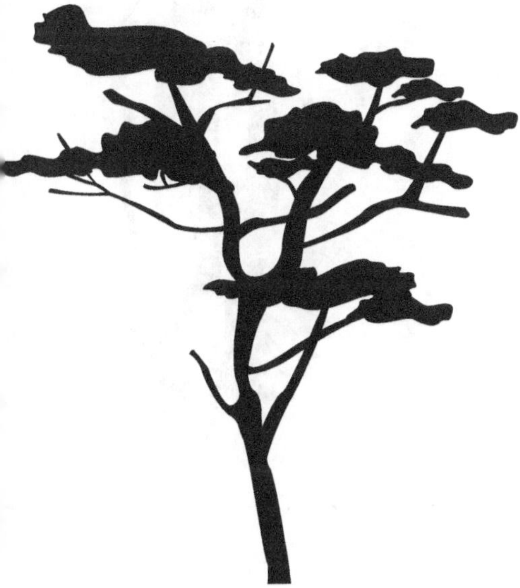

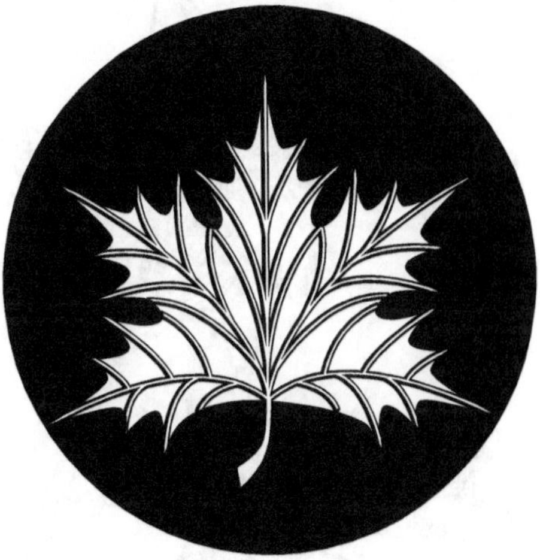

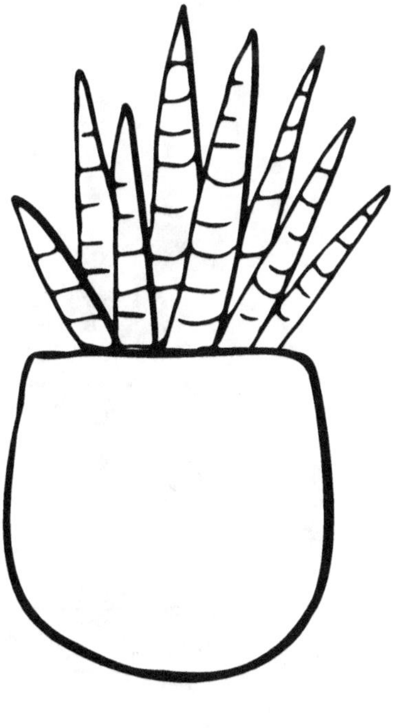

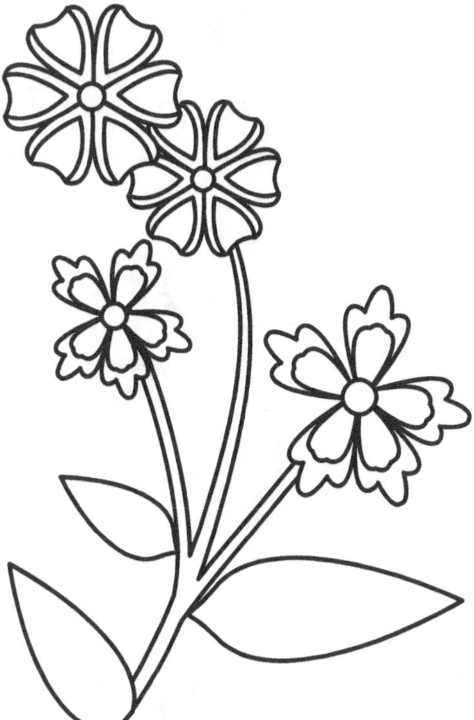

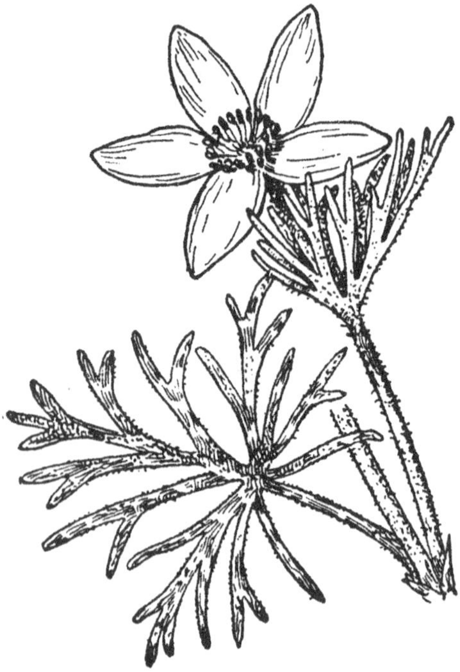
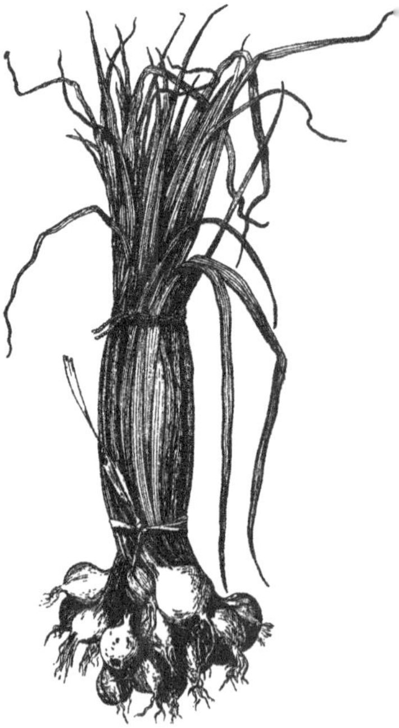
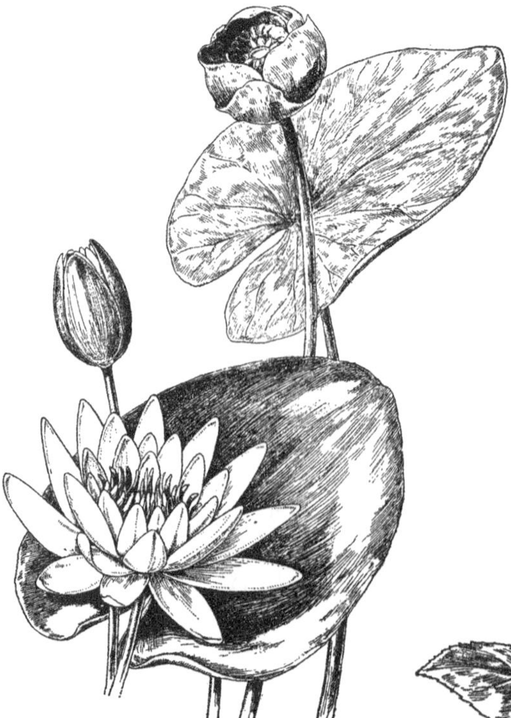
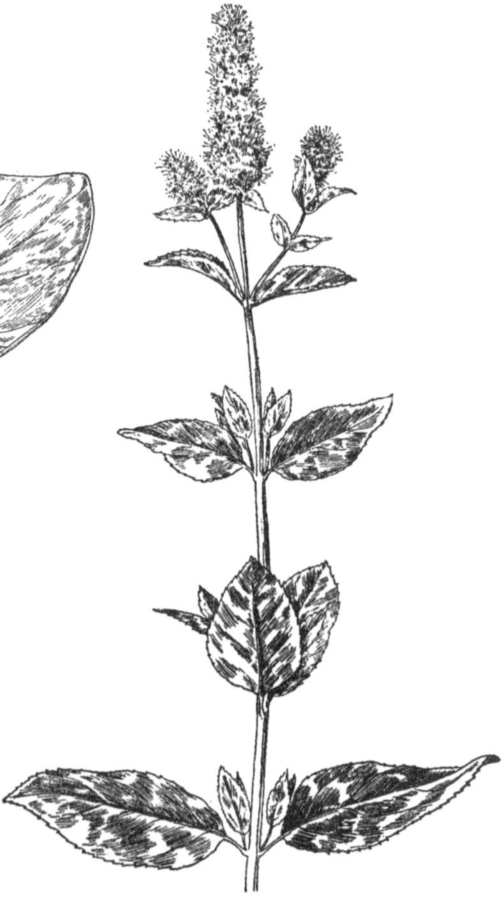

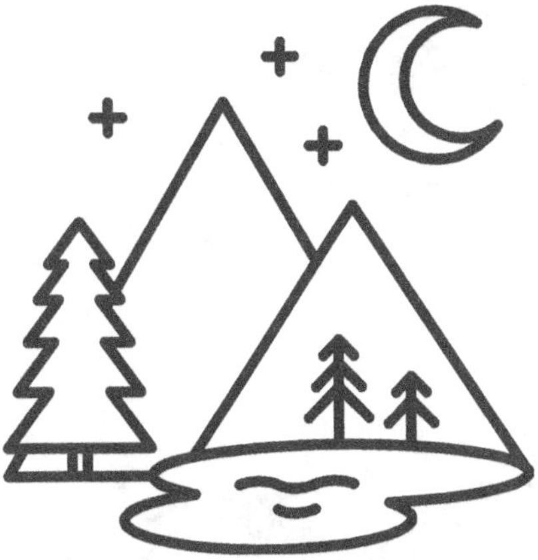

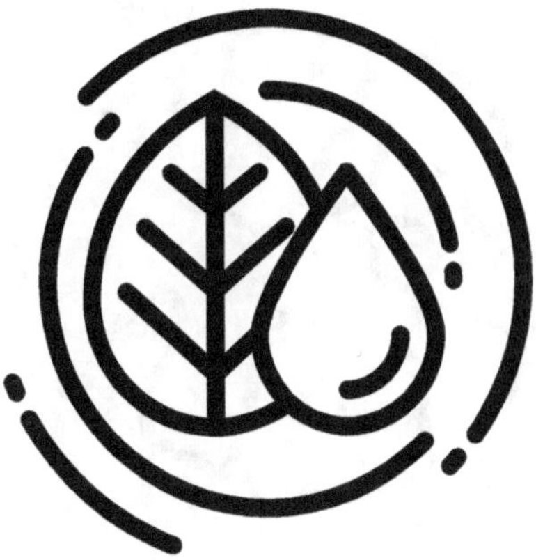

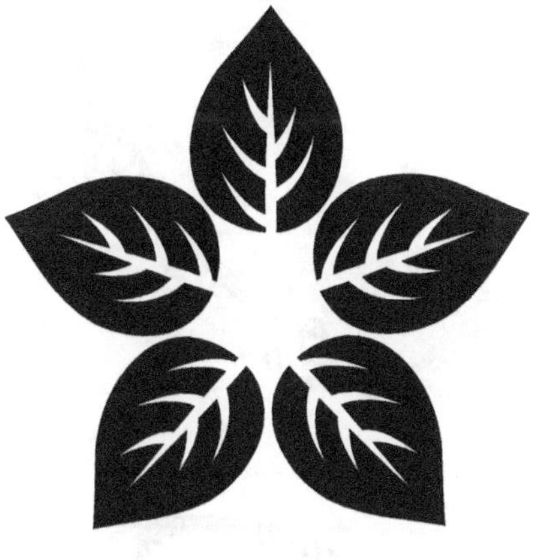

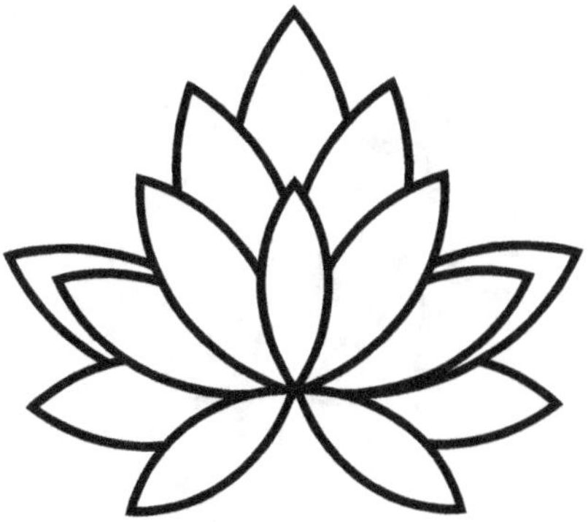

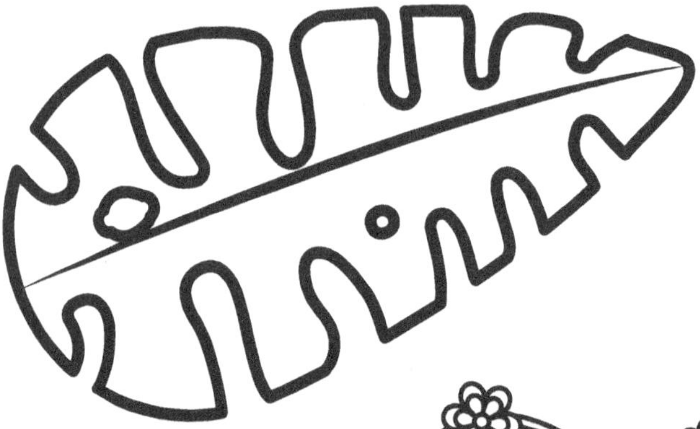
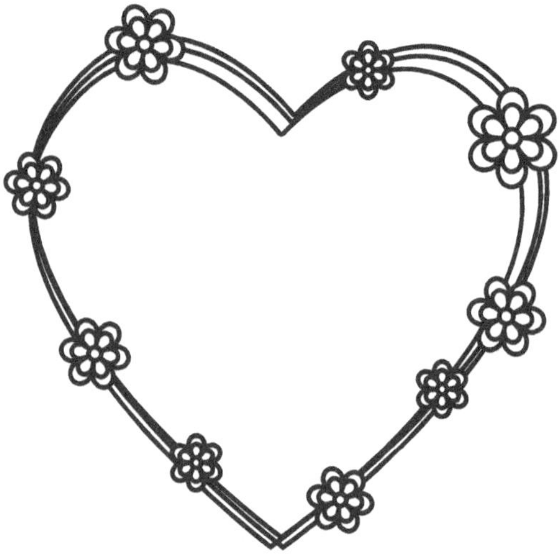
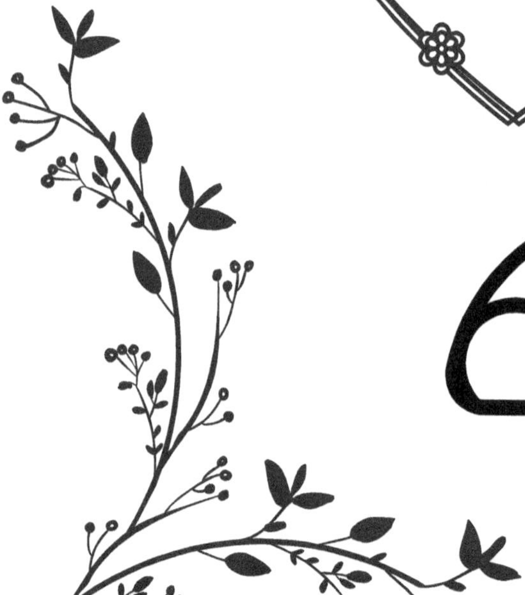
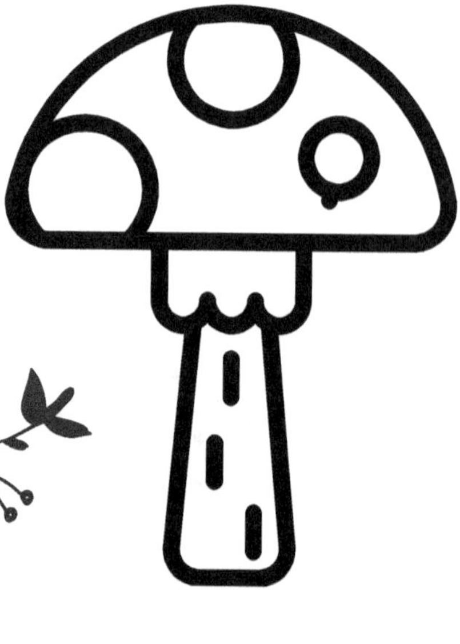

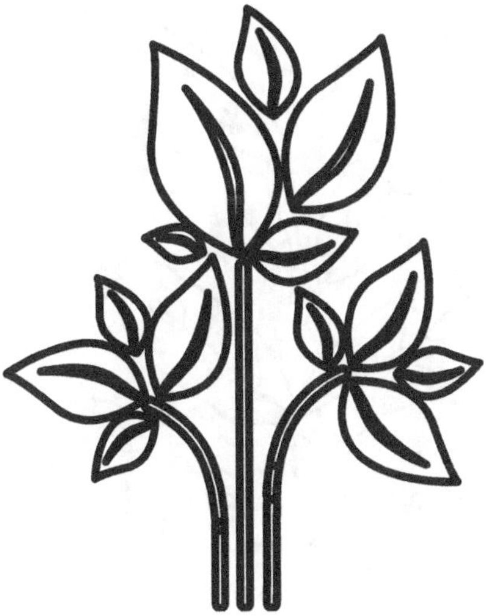

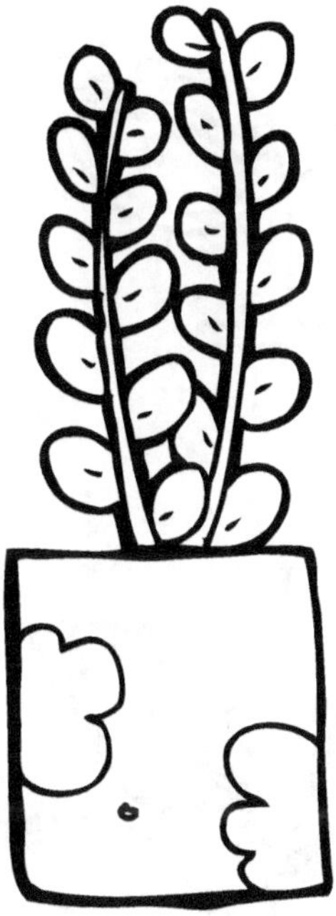

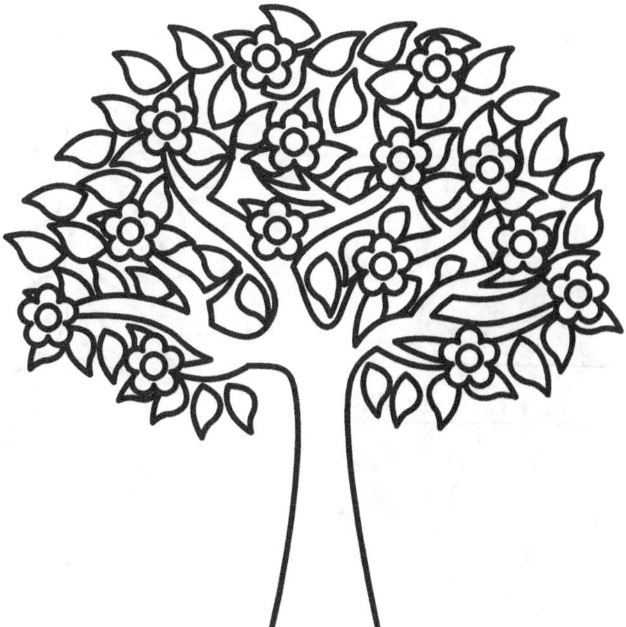

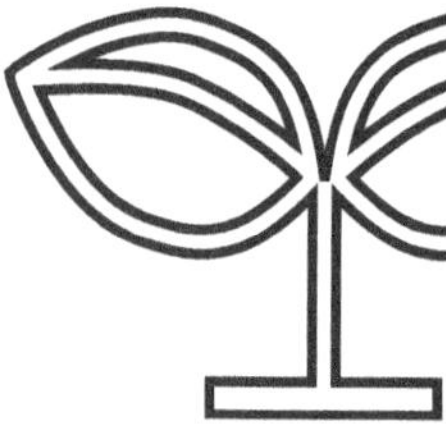
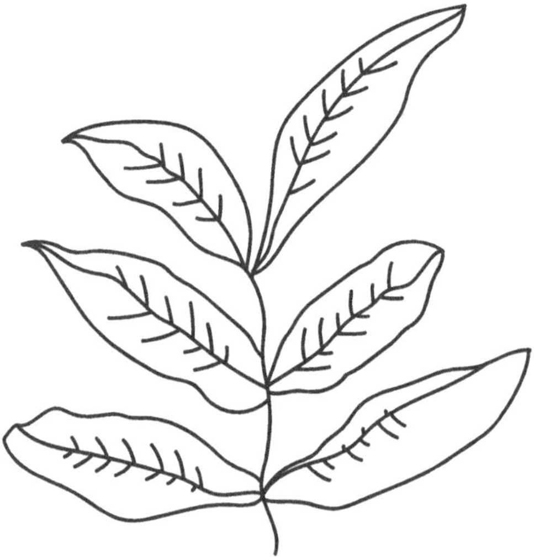
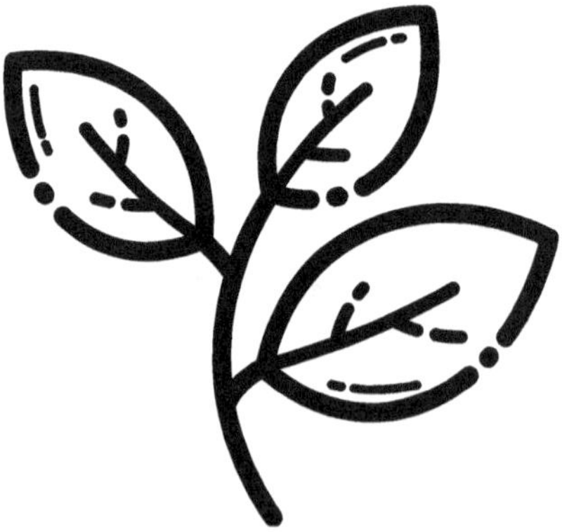

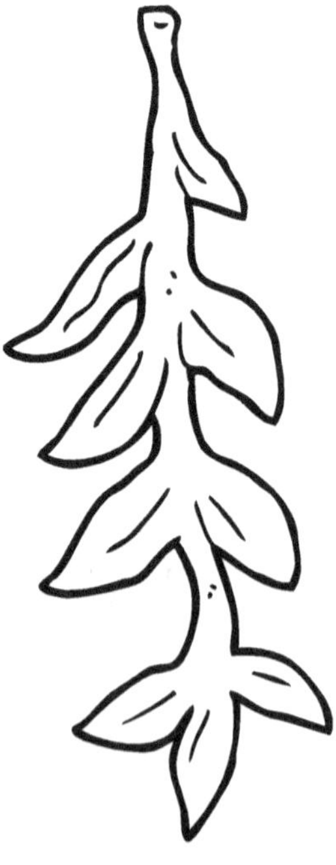

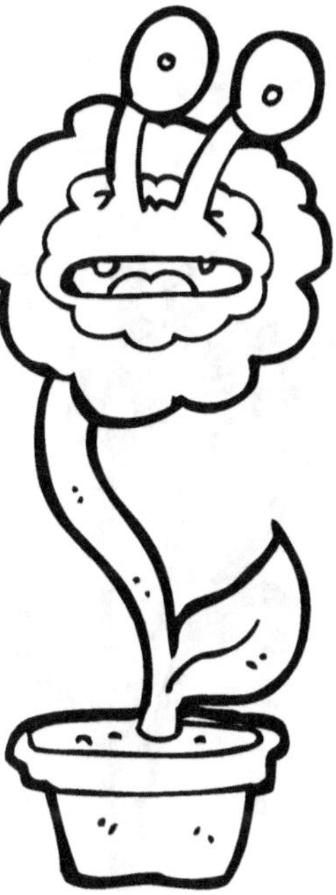
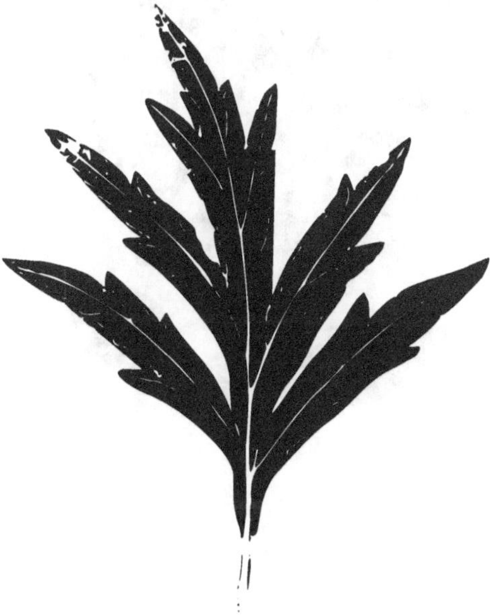
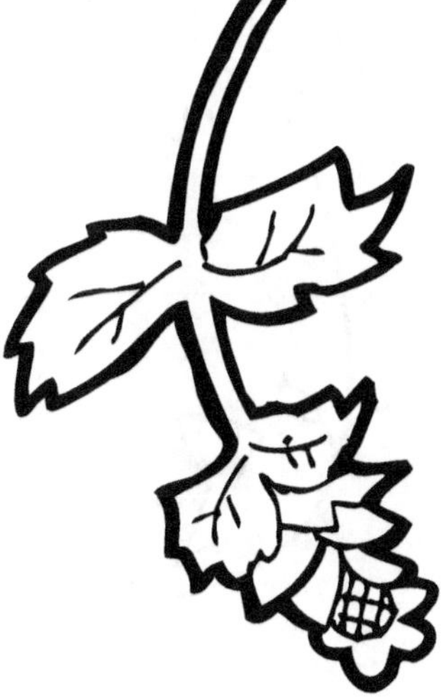
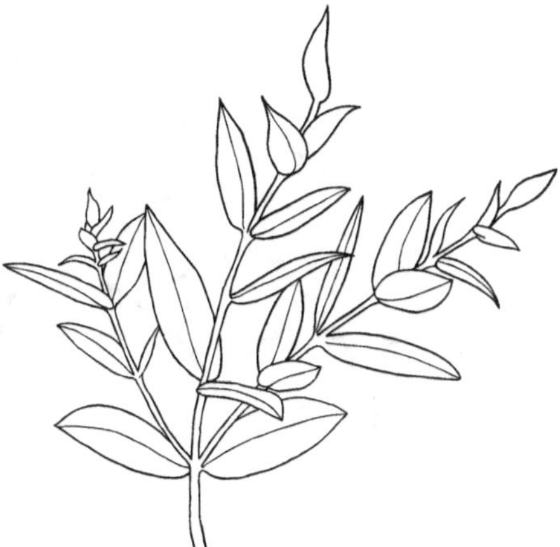

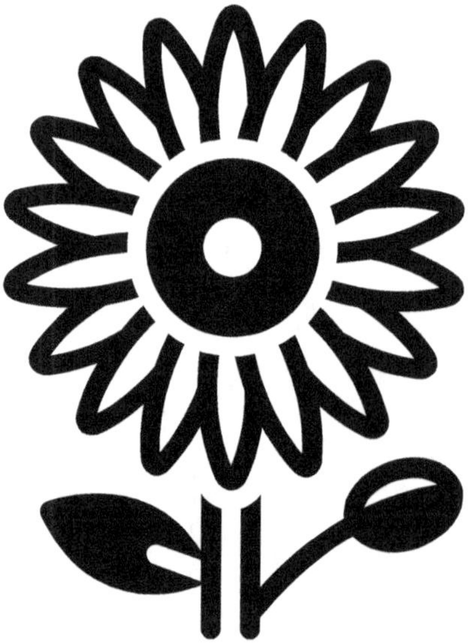

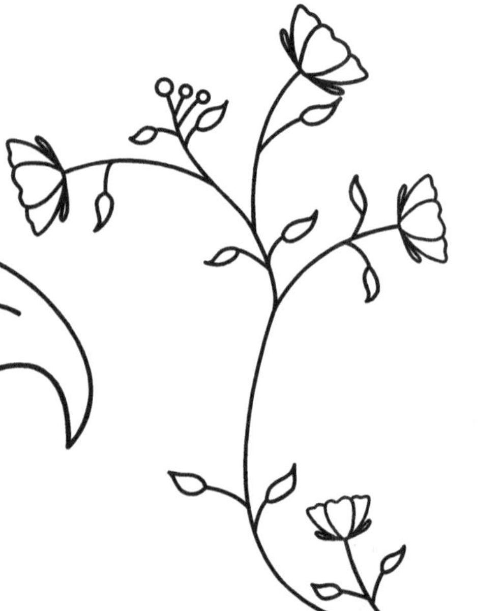

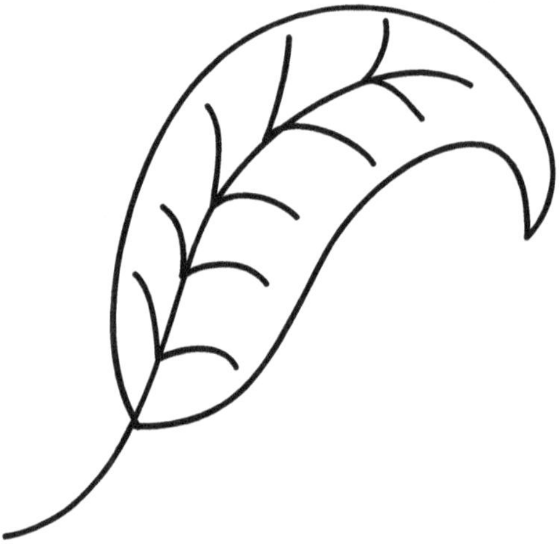

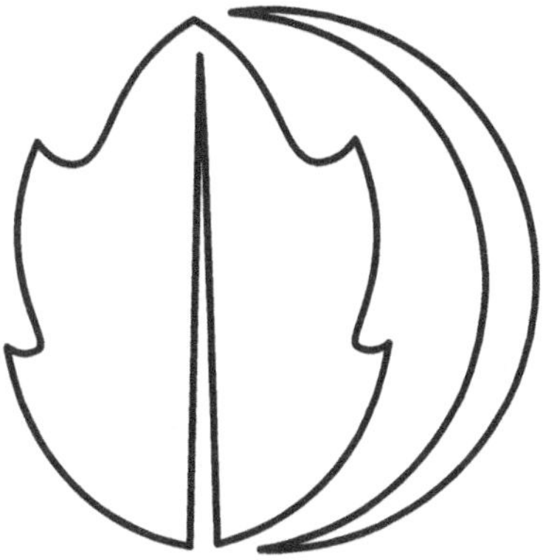

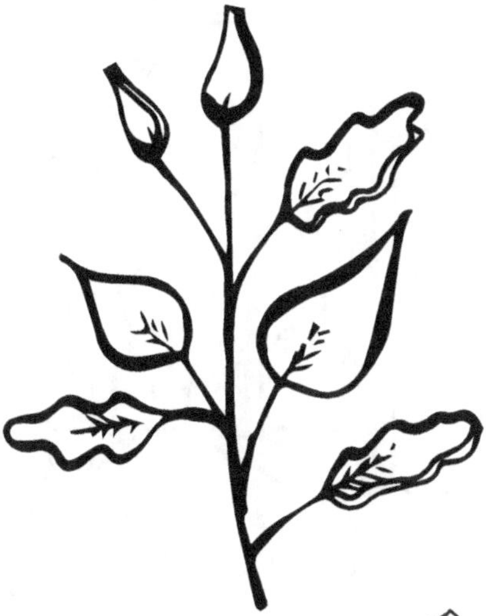

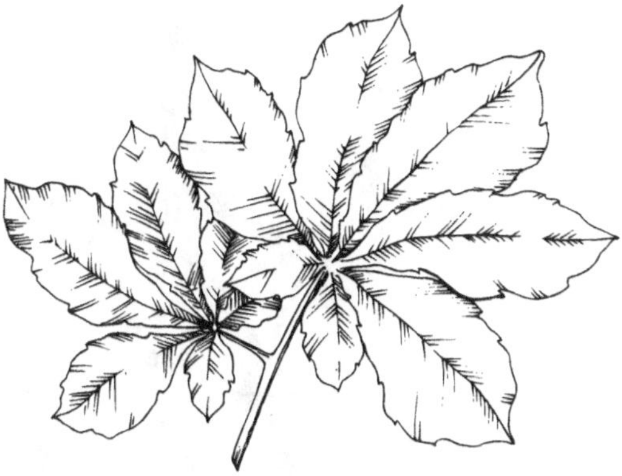

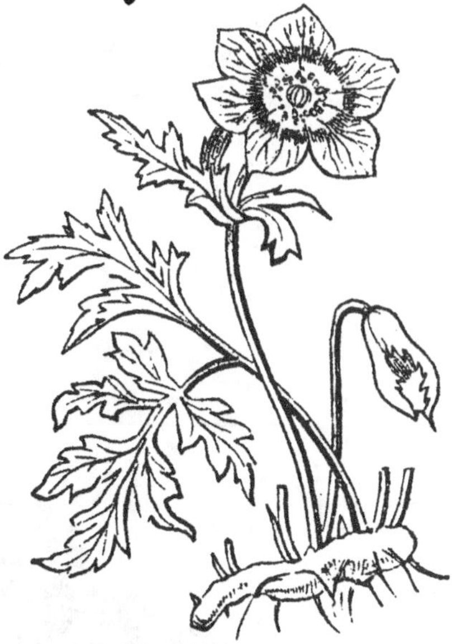

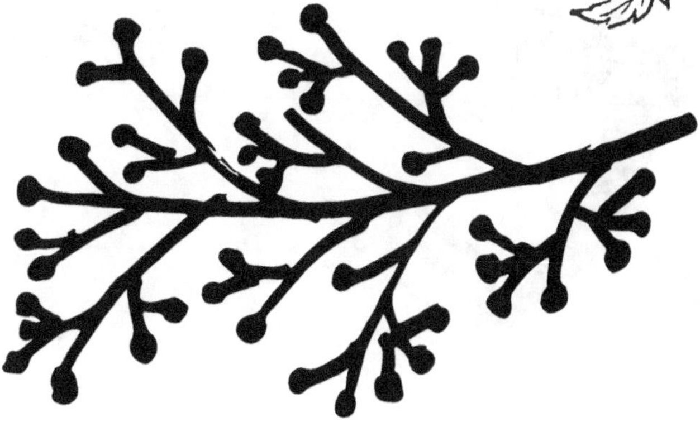

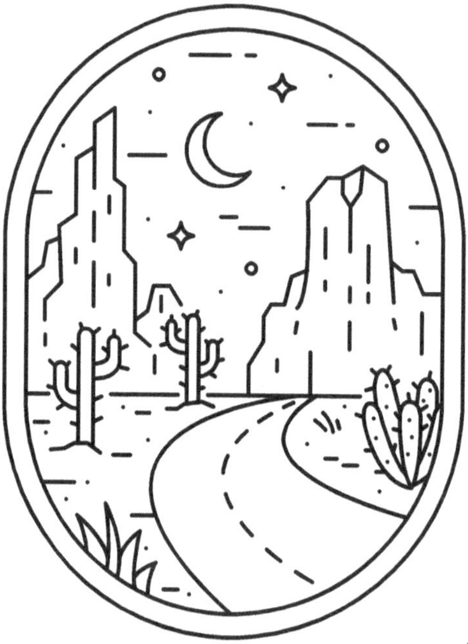

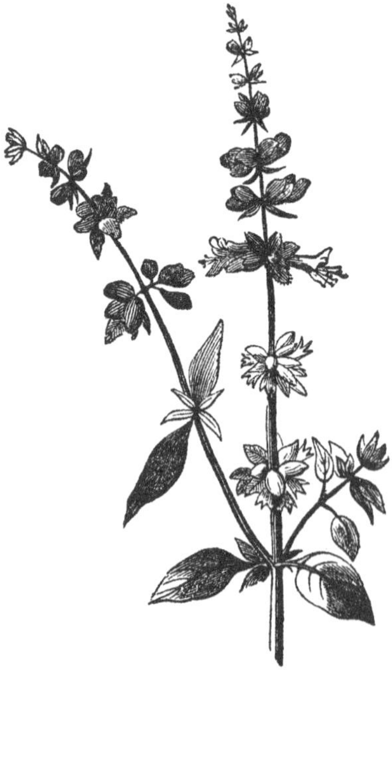

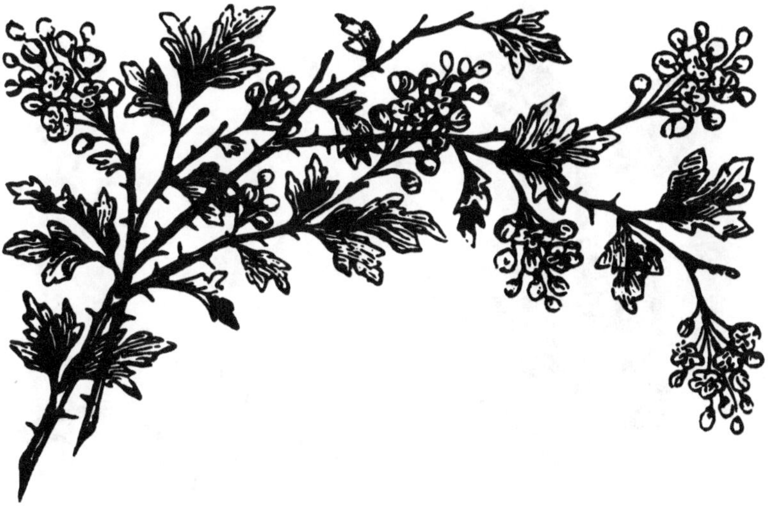

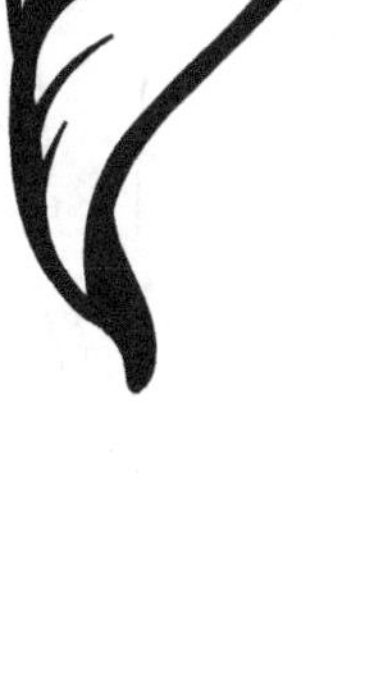

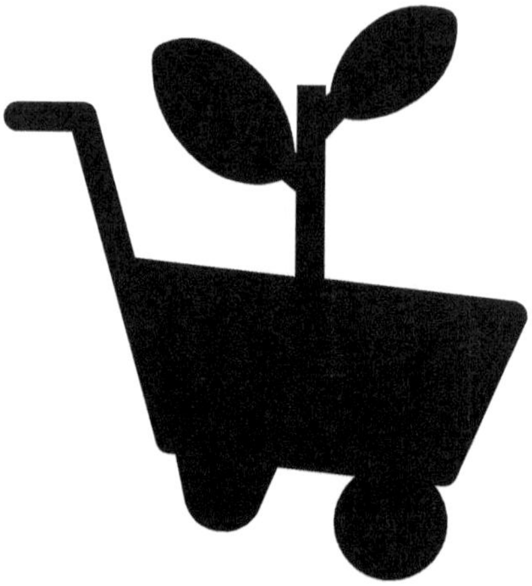

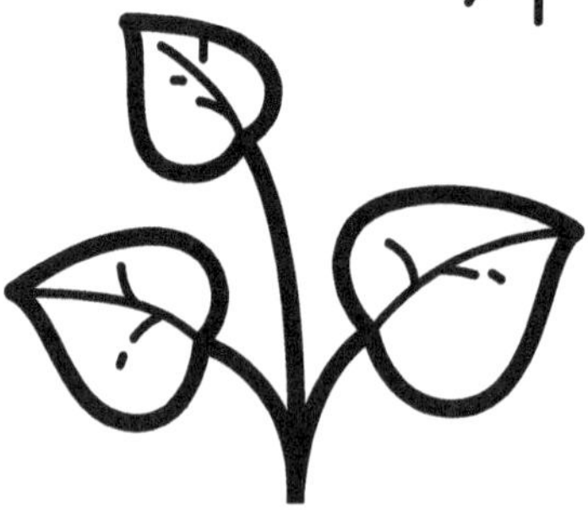

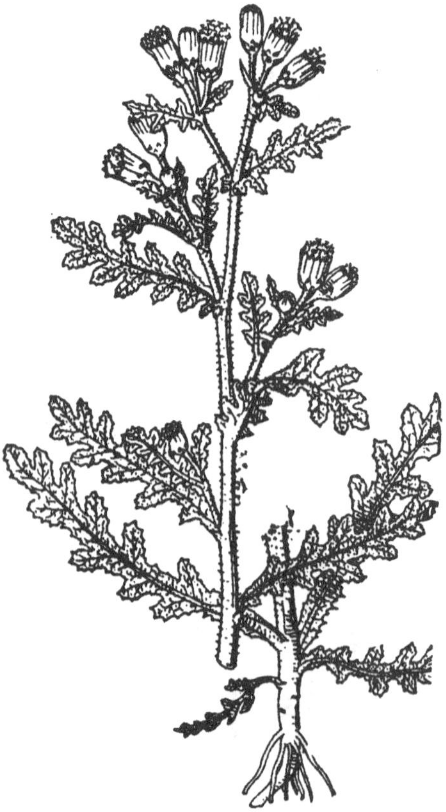

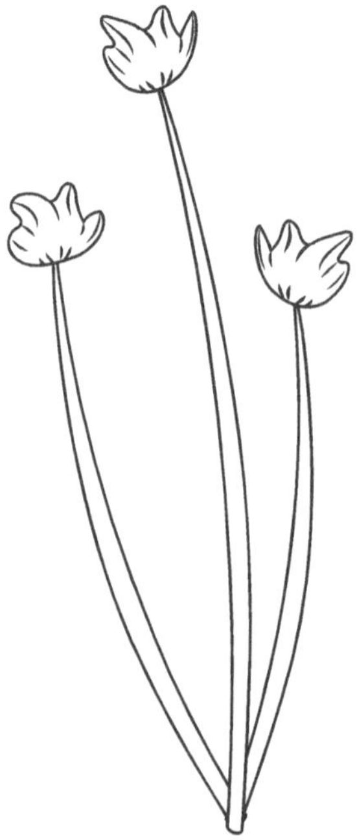

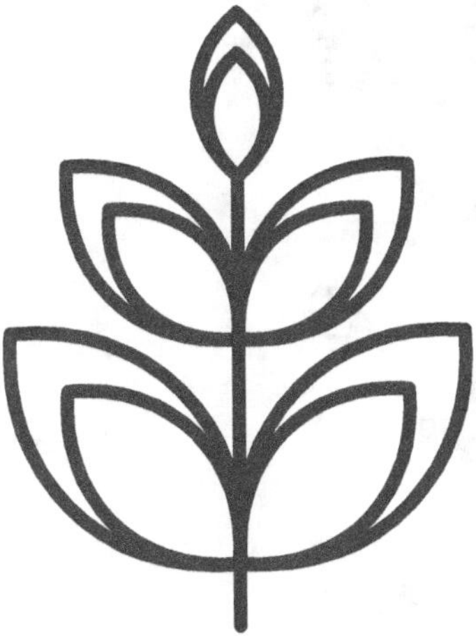

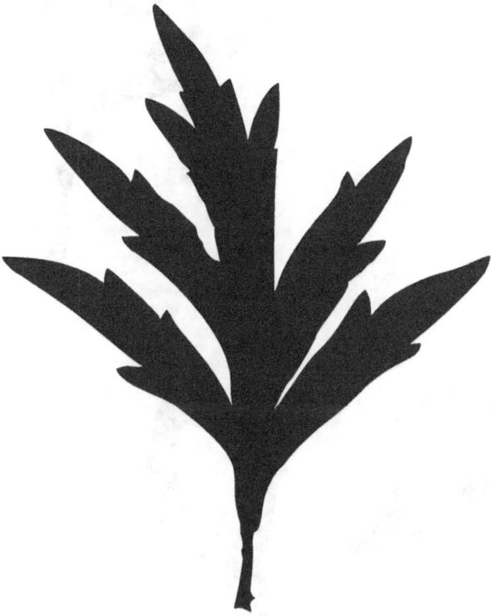

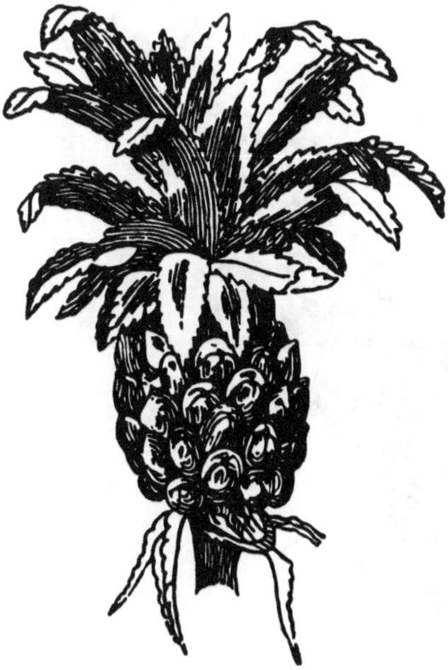

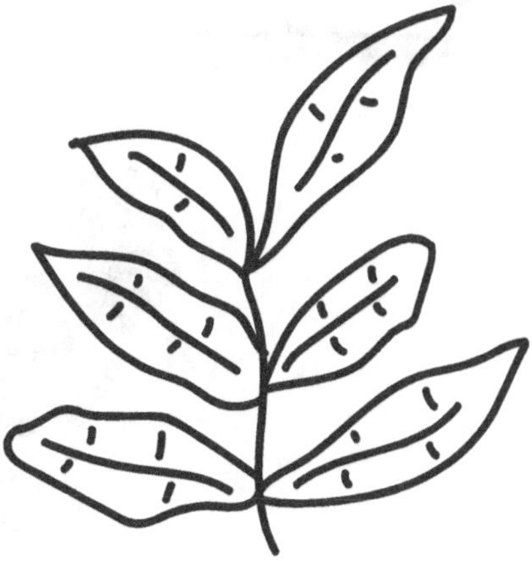

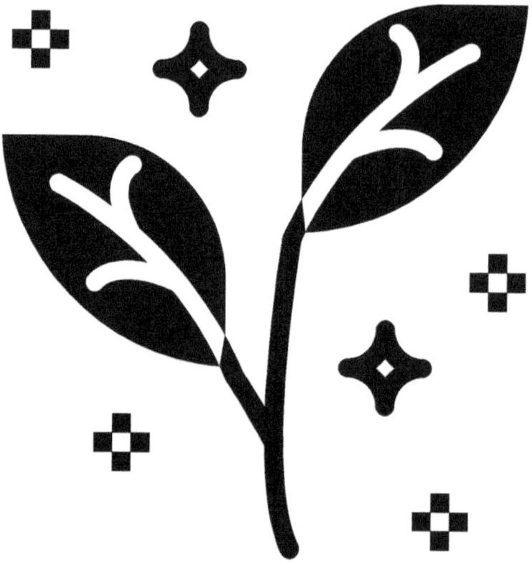

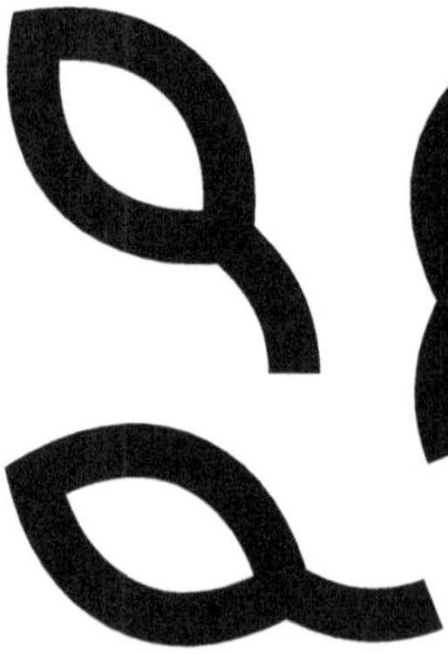

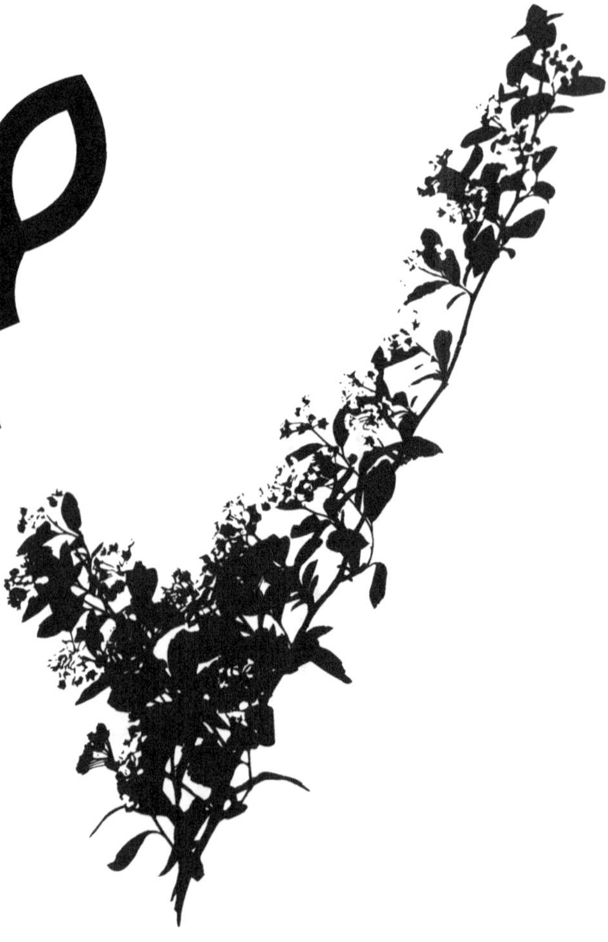

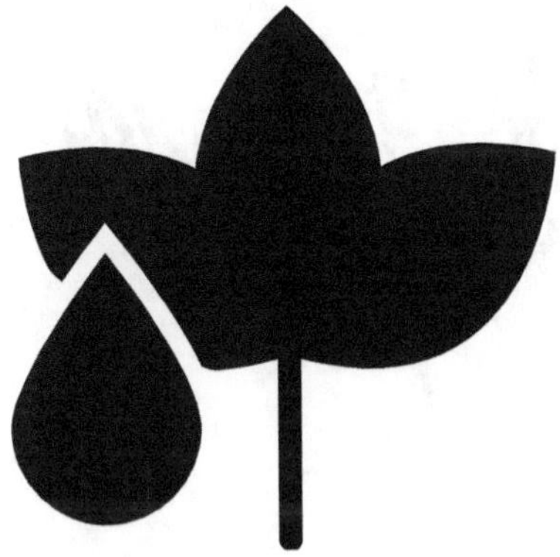

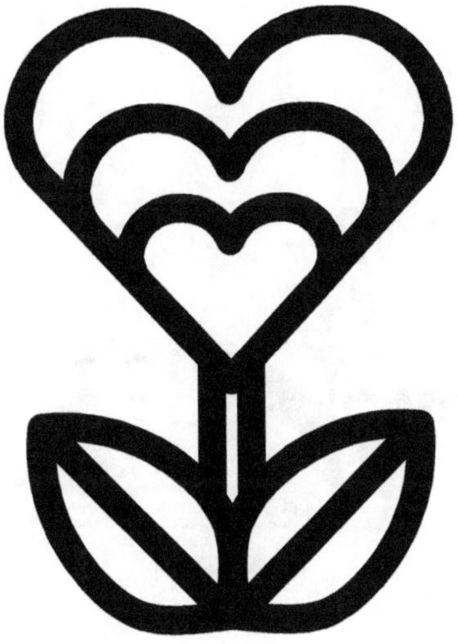

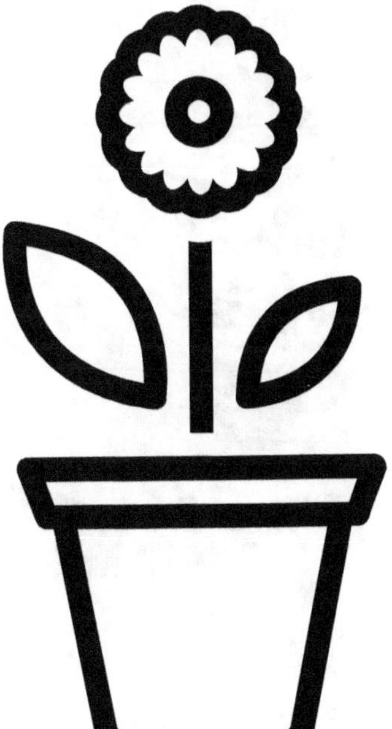

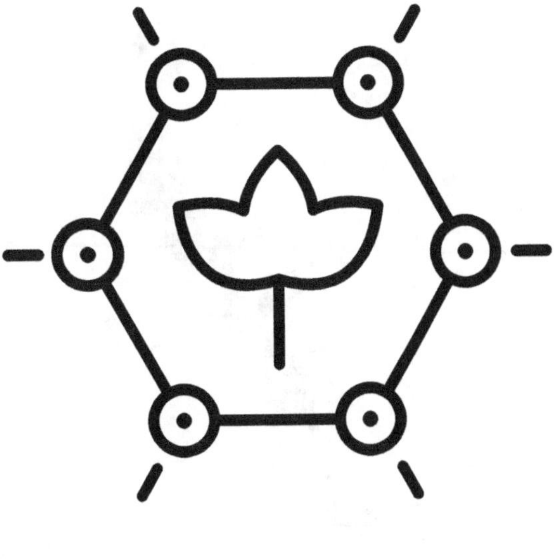

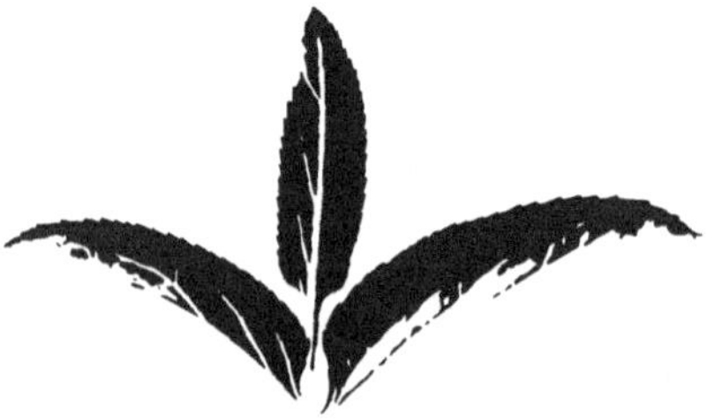

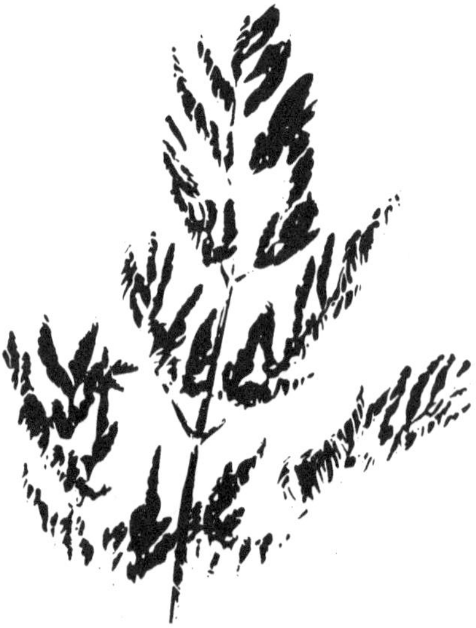

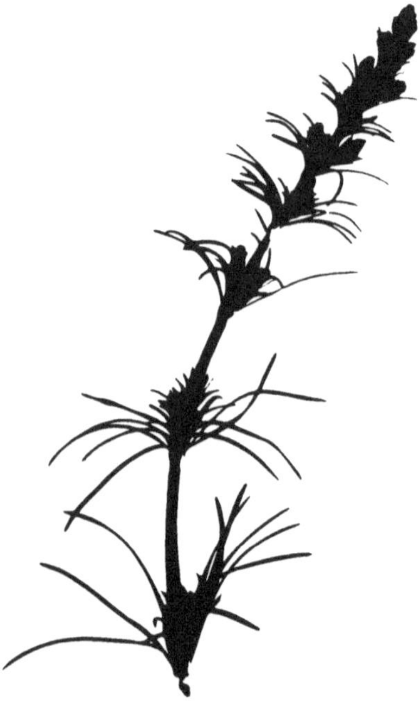

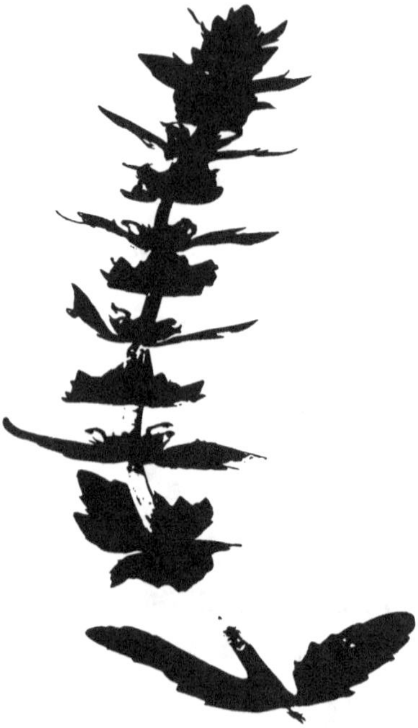

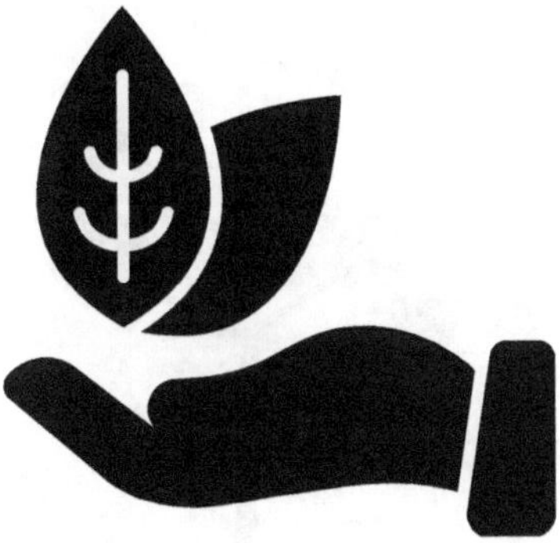

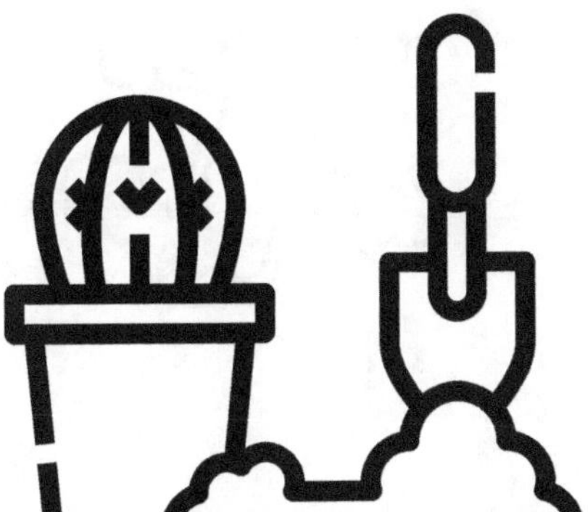

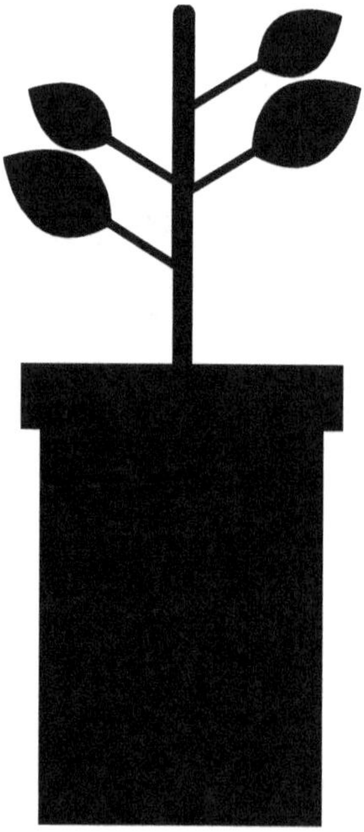
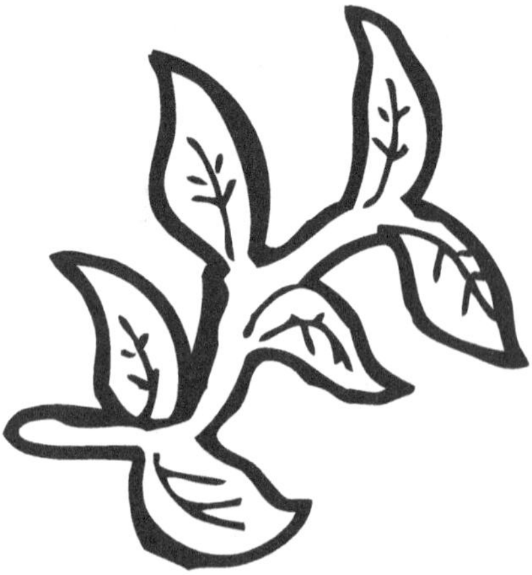
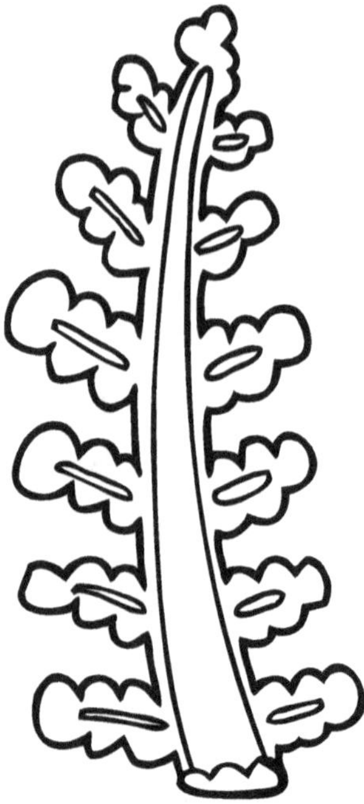
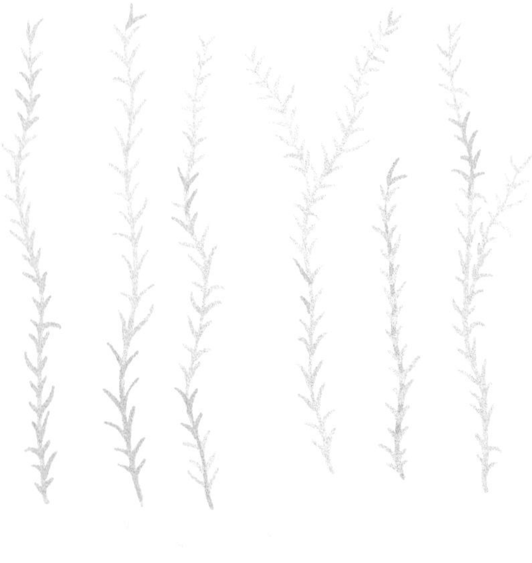

www.ingramcontent.com/pod-product-compliance
Lightning Source LLC
Chambersburg PA
CBHW070915220526
45466CB00005B/2221
9798532751408